# A Reflective
# Journey
## *of a Love One's*
# Passing

## CK Brashares

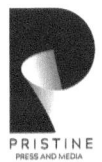

PRISTINE
PRESS AND MEDIA

ISBN
978-1-964804-73-6 (Paperback)
978-1-964804-72-9 (eBook)
978-1-964804-74-3 (Hardcover)

*A Reflective Journey of a Love One's Passing*

*CK Brashares*

# TABLE OF CONTENTS

# PROLOGUE

In our society, we are by social norms conditioned to view death as something to ignore, to dismiss, and to avoid discussing. I am sure that most people will not want to read this journey of death. I, for one, did not give the process much thought even though I went through a part of the process when our dad died. My siblings and I were with him in the hospital for a week as he lay in a coma, and we were there when he passed. Although the process of burying our dad fell on our mother's shoulders, had we known how emotionally and mentally challenging that process was, we would have offered our mother more help. It is my hopes that by reading this booklet, it will help you through this trying time and give you a look into what dying and death entail. It is important to remember not to deny your feelings: you are human, and you need to express them. At one time or another, you may feel angry with the person who is ill, you may feel like you cannot continue anymore, you may feel depressed, and you may feel deep sadness. However, instead of hiding from your feelings or stuffing them down inside yourself, which is well known to make you feel worse, express them in an appropriate way. If you have someone with whom you can talk about your thoughts and feelings, you will feel better and be more able to handle the end of your loved one's journey.

The idea for this book was born from my experience with my mother's journey into that good night. At 93, she found a lump in her left breast. Her oncologist found it was cancerous and that she also had cancer in both lungs. The doctor wanted to do a lung biopsy to confirm whether the breast and lung cancers were the same. However, he warned that the lung biopsy would be invasive and painful, and that chemotherapy was not recommended as it would likely kill her before the cancer did. He gave her six months to live. After taking in the doctor's findings and deciding she did not want to feel sicker, mom chose to do nothing. She said, "I want to enjoy my remaining days, doing what I love and remain as pain free as possible."

I now wish I had asked the hard question: "How did she feel about the death sentence?". From what I saw of her reaction, she just shrugged her shoulders and stared blankly at the doctor. She did not cry or seemed to react adversely to the news. To be fair, in her last few years, she often said she did not feel well and had been telling us since her late eighties, that she was "ready to go". Personally, I was glad that she chose not to have the biopsy or chemo. From what the doctor said, those procedures might have prolonged her life, but she would have been in pain and miserable. She lived two more years and passed away in August of 2021.

# A REFLECTIVE JOURNEY OF A LOVED ONE'S PASSING

by CK Brashares

# CHAPTER ONE

# MY EXPERIENCE

The one regret I have about the experience of my mother's illness and passing is that, in the end, I treated her like a two-year old and did not give her the respect owed a person with 95 years of lived wisdom. I felt sad when I became the parent and she the child in our relationship; when she could no longer hear to join in conversations; when her hands would not stop shaking and her eyes could not focus because of the morphine she was given for pain, which prevented her from being able to do hand embroidery—something that gave her joy and purpose. The thing that made me saddest was that, in her mind, she still viewed herself as capable, young, and viable, yet knowing that her perceptions did not match her body's realities any longer. I think for many of us that our perceptions of ourselves can be significantly different from how others perceive us. I could have been gentler in my approach to most of the areas she balked at, giving her the dignity that my mother deserved.

While in the midst of the experience, I thought that I was managing my emotions well. However, in the end, I realized that I was just fooling myself. Now, as I look back on this journey, I realize that even then I was moving through all the stages of grief.

- **Denial**: I could not believe the doctor when he told my mother that she had just six months to live. All indications were that she was still full of life and that it would take a lot to bring her down.

- **Anger:-**This stage was the sneakiest of all of them. I was not mad at the cancer, although I had good reason to be. What I realize now is that I was mad at my mother for stubbornly holding on to her right to eat what she wanted, sleep where she wanted, and manage this disease the way she wanted. I was mad that I had to treat her like a child because her decisions were not reasonable and doable. I was mad that she could not eat the food she liked, which led to wasted food because she could not or would not eat the food she was given. Most of all, I was mad at myself because toward the end I made my mother feel that her thoughts, feelings, and wishes were no longer considered and were dismissed. I had become the tyrant who took her dignity away.

- **Bargaining:** I do not know if I went through the bargaining stage. Since my mother was 93 at the time of diagnosis, she was going to pass either from cancer or old age, and there was no bargaining with that fact.

- **Depression:** At first, I did not think I was depressed, but as time passed and my thoughts dwelled on my mother's condition, many of my own pursuits fell by the wayside and opened the door to depression. I will talk about how depression affected me later in the book.

- **Acceptance:** Once I was honest with myself and my feelings, I was able to accept my mother's loss and begin to embrace the time I had left with her. I will mourn the loss of my mother, the person I could discuss sewing, embroidery, and crafts projects with, but will not cry over that loss. My mother left me many fond memories, gifts, and wisdom; she is the voice in my mind that I hear and will be with me forever. And now she is no longer in pain, for which I am thankful.

For myself, I do fear death and I don't equate a person leaving the physical realm with ceasing to exist. I do believe that we continue to exist, not in the same form, but that our energy is disbursed everywhere, and thus we see a wider view. I know this because of my uncle and his passing and the confirmation I received that he was okay.

My uncle contracted cancer later in life and it moved quickly through him. At the time, I was working as a freelance lithographer in my basement. Several weeks after I found out about my uncle's cancer, I experienced hearing a woman's voice telling me to pass on the message that his father loved him to my uncle. At first, I disregarded it as my imagination. From what I had heard about my uncle and his father, they had had a close relationship. However, the woman's voice persisted. Several weeks passed and the woman's voice was drowned out by a man's voice stating that message more emphatically to pass on the message of love. Finally, I relented and with fear and dread I went to see my uncle. Although I did tell him the message that his father loved him, I did not pass on the whole message. About six months later my uncle passed. The day of the funeral was incredibly sad because of his loss. I got home and felt tired, I took a nap, something that I normally do not do. I fell asleep almost immediately. I dreamt that I was in a sunlit, comfortable house and was walking through it. I went into the bedroom and up to a highboy dresser and pulled open a drawer. Within that drawer, I found a picture of my uncle and his father. His father had his arm around my uncle, and they both were smiling. I was no longer sad, because that was confirmation that my uncle and his father had reunited and that my uncle was happy.

Grief has a way of sneaking up on you when you least expect it and brings the remembrance of loved ones along with it. I came across a very cool embroidery or sewing item, I do not recall exactly what it was, but my first thought was that I needed to share it my mom. It took me back a bit, as I had to remind myself that she was gone. I am sure that the closer you were to a loved one, the stronger and more frequent this lapse of memory of their passing may be. Whatever you call it, this lapse of memory is overridden by a connection to a shared interest. Hence, a piece of clothing or a photograph is powerful enough to make you forget they are no longer here with you. And I am sure that it also brings pain along with it and you will momentarily relive the loss all over again. For some, this sharing, remembrance, and re-loss cycle may never be without pain, but for others it morphs into fond memories and brings other happy memories in their tow.

For myself, after the shock of remembrance comes the peace that she is no longer in pain and the knowledge that she would have liked what I was going to show her. Now my task is to move forward with my life, live it fully, appreciate her special place in my life, and remember all the wonderful gifts she gave me. By reliving those memories without sorrow but with the same joy as she lived her life, I honor her.

In another view, my sister is not afraid either. In her belief system, my mother is with Jesus. I know there are many who feel the same and I am glad that they have that belief within them as it does comfort them. I cannot help thinking of the many people who don't share that view or, worse, have no belief system in place. It must be a scary thing for them.

My view regarding death was shaped by how my parents managed it, my belief system and what I experienced through outside influences. One that stands out in my mind was an episode on the Twilight show narrated by Rod Sterling. In an episode, a young man (Robert Redford) was seen on several occasions by an old woman. He always smiled at her but never approached as she seemed very afraid of him. I do not remember the reason, but he finally came to her door, and she would not let him in. He tried several times but got the same response each time. Finally, she let him into her home and was not afraid anymore. At this point, the shot pans to her lifeless body lying on her bed. This is when you find out that Robert Redford was death and that is why the old woman was afraid of him. However, in the end, she accepted him and was no longer fearful. To some this was a morbid premise/show, but it stuck with me. I found it profound that when we finally let go, there is nothing to fear. However, that is the Catch 22 of the situation: in order to be less fearful or non-fearful, the situation calls for complete resignation to the event, which is the crux of the matter.

It is my fervent wish, dear reader, that you may find peace from the loss of your loved one, your pain will diminish, and that time will bring you only fond, loving memories and joy of having them in your life.

The following chapters describe my personal journey, thoughts, and feelings during the last two years of my mother's life. I bare my feelings to you about this journey in the hopes that it will be helpful in some way as you go through similar circumstances. Everyone's journey will be different, as will the medical condition (be it cancer or something else) and how it affects you and your loved one. What remains a constant is the emotional impact this disease and a loved one's passing have on all of us.

CHAPTER TWO

# THE DIAGNOSIS

I remember the day my mother called me. She rarely called me, relying on me to initiate conversation. I can count on the one hand the number of times she called me since I married and moved into my own home. She said, "I found a lump in my left breast, can you call to make an appointment with my doctor?" For some time now I had started to dread taking my mother to the doctor or anywhere, for that matter. She had bouts of incontinence so does not like to go out. It was like she had a hollow leg filled with liquid. Anytime we took her anywhere, bathroom breaks became a high priority. For example, my sister took her to Jo-Ann Fabrics, a place she liked to visit and over the course of the hour she was in the store, she had to use the bathroom four times. Because of that, she never got to see anything but the bathroom. I should state that mom did wear an incontinence panty but could not bring herself to void into it. That process is so ingrained in us that it is difficult to accept when the body no longer supports us holding our liquids back.

Of course, I made the appointment with her primary doctor, and they got her in right away. Upon examination of her left breast, her doctor confirmed her findings that she indeed had a mass within that breast. The doctor needed more information to determine what medical procedure to follow, so he ordered an ultrasound to find out how large the mass was.

The doctor set up the appointment for the following week. We got to the appointment extra early— arriving everywhere excessively early was another of my mom's traits that drove me crazy— and the ultrasound scan confirmed that there was a mass there about 3 centimeters (1.18 inches) long and about 2.0 centimeters (0.8 inches) wide. Her physician advised her to have a biopsy done to determine if the mass was cancerous, which she agreed to do. She wanted to know herself. When the day came to have the biopsy done, she was so nervous. I do not know where she was holding the liquid that came out of her that day, but she had to use the bathroom seven times while we were there. What bothered me was not the fact that she had to go to the bathroom so often but maneuvering the wheelchair around to get her there. When you need to use the facilities, you do not want to have to wait until the chair gets into position so you can go.

It was approximately two weeks before the biopsy results came back and, yes, it was cancerous. Her primary doctor could not do anything more for her, so he set up an appointment with an oncologist that he recommended.

We had to wait the longest for this appointment, about two months. At this appointment, the cancer doctor examined her breast again but wanted more information. He ordered a CT (computed tomography) scan which would give a better look at the lump. So, back to the hospital we went. Mom was not keen on having to take the chalky-tasting dye drink so the doctors could see her breast and lump more clearly. She had had a previous experience with a dye drink and had trouble getting it down. Recalling that experience her body shook. Thank goodness for progress. Although the drink was still unpleasant to drink, they had improved the taste greatly, according to mom.

When the results came back, the CT scan revealed that she had two spots, one in each lung, along with the tumor in her left breast. The spot on her left lung was larger than the one on her right lung.

It is my opinion that we are conditioned to think that doctors can treat or fix pretty much anything these days. However, we do not always think about what those treatments do to patients. Most, though necessary, can be painful; in some cases, they can cause death. I was really impressed with the cancer doctor, because he treated my mother like his own mother, which I appreciated. He explained to us that a lung biopsy would have to be done to determine if the cancer in her breast and lung were of the same type. However, due to mom's advanced age of 93, the doctor said that while a lung biopsy would be a recommended procedure, if it was his mom, he would not do it because the procedure is very painful, and it might kill her in the process. The other option, of course, was chemotherapy and that was just as dangerous at her advanced age. After explaining the options and drawbacks, the doctor asked mom if she wanted to pursue either of these treatments. She chose the third option— to do nothing. She said she would rather feel mostly well rather than sick. I was glad that she chose this option because I knew if she had chosen the other option (to go through a lung biopsy or chemo) that she would have been miserable and would have made us miserable too.

And yes, in my opinion, it is okay to feel this emotion, as you are only human. If you start denying the feelings that come up when dealing with your loved one's challenging time, you might start feeling depressed, which is anger turned inward and can make you sick eventually. You do not want your energy to be so low that you are not able to help your loved one, creating a vicious cycle. Denial is not your friend at this point. I think you will find that your loved one will appreciate your honesty and it will help open them up to share what they are feeling. Talking though the challenges of the illness, and all the fears and concerns will benefit you and your loved one, especially if sprinkled with a bit of humor if you can manage it.

Since she had chosen not to take any means of prolonging her life, mom asked the doctor how long she had to live. He gave her six months. By her demeanor, mom seemed resigned to her fate. I did not have the guts to ask her how she felt about the diagnosis, so I can only surmise there was shock and disbelief going through her mind. For myself, I was in shock and initially did not feel any emotion. I could not grasp the idea that she would be gone within a few months because she was still so vibrant and full of life. She did not look like a person who had cancer. However, my mom was a survivor and would continue fighting, even though she was feeling pain. That was just her way and her makeup as a person. The fact that she wanted to go home right away was the only "tell" about what she was feeling in that moment, as normally she would have wanted to go out to lunch afterward.

Her last appointment with the cancer doctor was June 24, 2018. The doctor placed an order for hospice to come in to help mom through the ending journey of her life. She received a call from hospice about two weeks later. They said they would come to the house and would do an evaluation to see if she was a candidate for their service.

## Hospice

When the hospice nurse came to mom's house, she was pleasant, helpful, and informative. She explained what hospice would and could do for mom. For example, they would be there 24/7 if the doctor prescribed the need for their service. She made it clear that they do not offer medical preventive care but only offer comfort level assistance (palliative care). Although the oncologist referred mom, this visit was an evaluation to determine if mom was a viable candidate for their service. By the end of the evaluation, the hospice nurse said that mom was a definite candidate for hospice services.

The nurse asked her:

- Are you able to cook for yourself?
- Are you able to wash or shower by yourself?
- Are you able to get dressed by yourself?

At the time of the evaluation, my mom answered yes to the last two and no to the first question. My mom could no longer stand long enough to cook her meals. However, it took longer to do so. Mom was still able to dress herself and, with minimal help from my sister who lived with her, get into the shower.

During this meeting, the nurse began planning for mom's care. The hospice nurse went on to ask about **the diagnosis, symptoms, discomfort, current medications, and health history** to better understand mom's concerns and determine how the hospice team could help.

Also, any of mom's prescription needs would be managed and delivered by hospice, which would work closely with and be in regular contact with mom's main physician. Hence, if mom needed her meds renewed or modified, hospice would contact her physician and the doctor would write a new script, which hospice would fill and send directly to the house. Since mom was homebound, this was a nice service.

Due to mom's diminishing immune system, she developed cellulitis on her lower legs. Cellulitis is a bacterial infection in the deep layers of skin that occurs after a break in the skin or an insect bite. Hospice provided all the wraps, ointments, and supplies needed to take care of this problem. Their main aim was to keep mom as comfortable as possible for as long as possible, which they did very well and with compassion.

Hospice service, in the area in which I reside, not only includes nursing care but also a home worker, a spiritual person, a massage therapist, and a social worker who are all involved with your loved one's care. This first week you will be busy talking with a spiritual leader of your faith; a person to help with dressing, bathing, and the general needs of your loved one; a social worker to help with any financial assistance or specialized needs your loved one may have, and a massage therapist to help address your loved one's sore muscles from sitting or reclining for long periods.

My mother was a Catholic and they sent out a priest who listened to her confession, which my mom appreciated. Although she saw each hospice team member initially, she refused further visits from the health worker and massage therapist. Mom felt that she did not need massaging or having someone help her dress, and she was adamant that she could take a shower by herself. Although her children did not agree with that assumption, some battles are better not fought.

The social worker turned out to be mom's nephew's wife, so she accepted her help but not for what she stood for. Her job was to coordinate the others on the team assigned to mom, assess their helpfulness to mom, and to provide financial assistance and information. Mom did not need the financial help but did ask for help to check on benefits from the Veterans Affairs, as my dad had been a veteran.

Overall, I have to say that I was impressed by the hospice service and how well they strove to make my mom's last days comfortable, enjoyable, and as stress free as possible. The care they provided was exceptional, compassionate, and loving.

CHAPTER THREE

# THE WAITING

I prepared myself for mom's inevitable demise and gathered the strength to go through her many wants and desires while we traveled this road. I wondered what other people did or felt, as a loved one slowly diminished. Did they feel the weight of seeing that person slowly turn physically, mentally, and visually into someone they no longer recognized? I thought about how difficult, lonely, and sad that must be for those going through this process and those who have to witness it. My thoughts went to my own mother, the person the dying process was happening to, and wondered how she felt. I missed a wonderful opportunity to find out by simply asking her, but I chickened out. I asked her the simple question, "How are you feeling today" and she would answer "Not so well." That was her physical feeling, not the emotional and mental feelings that I really wanted to know. I also wondered if she was scared. I wanted to know how she felt about her coming end. I did have glimpses into her mindset when one day she stated, "God must not want me or is mad at me, because he has not come for me yet. Why has God not come for me?" She asked this question early in the second year before she passed.

Mom had trouble sleeping prone in her bed. She said it was because her left leg, which had a knee replacement in her eighties, was too heavy and she could not find a comfortable place to rest it. Instead, mom was used to sitting up and sleeping in her recliner 24/7. However, she would not put her feet up to relieve the pressure on her legs.

We had gotten an adjustable hospital bed and placed it in the living room so she could sleep as well as watch TV. However, she did not like the mattress. While she did try to sleep in the bed, she could not get comfortable so for six months it sat in the living room unused.

I felt so sad for my mom and how her body was betraying her at every level. She was fearful to go out due to her incontinence and her hearing loss. Her pain weighed heavily on me, making me feel sad, although I did not recognize it right away. Before I realized what it was that I was feeling, I felt quite tired and no longer wanted to do the things I normally did. Eventually I realized I was depressed from the constant immersion in my mom's daily diminishing life. My mom kept up a good front, mostly for her children, and maintained a happy demeanor. However, every once in while her mask would slip, and you could see her anger with her situation weighing on her mind. I think the hardest part of the entire process, dying and aging, is the part where you can no longer do the simple things for yourself. She did not want to take a shower, because it made her feel colder than she already did, and she had trouble getting into the shower from her walker. Sometime at the beginning of the second year, I had my husband take out the shower door. We then installed a curved shower curtain rod and a shower curtain. This change made it easier for mom to access the shower.

She could no longer cook for herself because she could not stand long enough to complete a meal. This, I feel, saddened, and angered her the most, as she was an exceptional cook. She cooked all her meals from scratch with good healthy ingredients. She could no longer call and speak with anyone, even her sister, because her hearing loss was so bad. In her eighties, she took up hand embroidery again to tame the trembling in her right hand. However, between her diminishing eyesight and the trembling of her hands, toward the end she could no longer do the thing she loved the most, hand embroidery.

She also started to have trouble eating. Foods that previously had tasted good to her no longer did. My mother was very opinionated and an exceptionally good cook, so the food had to be familiar and taste good. More to the point, it had to taste like she had made it. This was a very tough thing to do. First, no one cooks the same. You do not buy the same ingredients and your cooking sense is different. My poor sister was at her wits end trying to appease mom's taste buds and tummy, which fought each other. We all did the best we could.

My mother had five children. Evelyn, who still worked and was the next to youngest, lived with our mother and had to endure her many mood swings, temper tantrums, and her eating wants and dislikes. Our brother R.J. came out on Mondays to visit with mom and bring her lunch. I came out on Tuesdays. Denise, who also still worked, came on Wednesdays to have lunch with her. Tina (the youngest) came on weekends to visit and fix mom's meals. We were lucky that each of us was willing to help and contribute. I do not know how some families, who only have one or two children, handle the care of elderly loved ones— especially when they can no longer cook for themselves or do simple household chores or, worse, cannot take showers by themselves.

For the last 10 years, my mother and I had had lunch together every Tuesday. She liked to have something brought in from a restaurant. The first year-and-a-half after her diagnosis, she was able to eat what she requested. Going into the last six months of her life, I think morphine, the cancer, and the antibiotics she took changed her taste buds. Because food that she had liked before started to taste funny to her, and because her stomach became so sensitive to certain foods, she could not eat them.

Even as my mother's physical capabilities deteriorated, her mindset stayed strong. When mom received her diagnosis, I thought this was going be a long haul because her mind was still capable, quick, and you could not trick her. But as her body slowly failed her, her legs grew weak and developed cellulitis, and she suffered severe hearing loss. As her hearing failed, my role became more pronounced and the shift from child to adult became more apparent. She still could make reasonable decisions but would latch onto them like a bulldog and you could not budge her. It was like she understood somewhere in her mind the situation before her but if she did not like the events or likely outcome, she would change the information or scenario to her desired outcome. She would constantly tell any new person coming in to care for her, that she had high blood pressure and did not have it previously. She wondered why she had to take medicine for it, although she had had this condition for over 15 years. Also, hospice started prescribing a pediatric dosage (0.25 milliliters) of oral morphine to help calm her and alleviate any discomfort she had. She would only take it when she absolutely could not stand the pain any longer. The nurses told her repeatedly that she would not get addicted to it because her body would not react to it in that way. Morphine had a purpose within her body and her body would use it differently than someone ingesting it for pleasure. Regardless, she could not be convinced of that fact. Eventually, toward the end, she changed her position and took a daily dose to help ease the pain that she was experiencing.

In the last six months of her life, mom showed signs of diminishing mobility when trying to get up out of the recliner to use the bathroom. In the last month before her passing, this ability diminished markedly. Toward the end mom had to be helped up and out of the recliner and escorted to the bathroom. This meant that someone had to stay near her during the day. We were so afraid she might fall and break a bone, which would have made her even more miserable. When it became apparent that we could no longer help her get in and out of the recliner, she finally had to go to the adjustable bed. She was moved into bed on a Friday. The hospice nurses placed a catheter in her and put her into the bed, where she immediately fell asleep. I remember thinking as they helped her into the bed how exceedingly small and hunched over, she looked. In the last two months of her life, she aged dramatically. Before the cancer, my mother still had some brown color to her hair, but that day I only saw very grey/white hair. Three days later in the wee hours of the morning, she died.

It was like she had given up. While she was in the recliner sitting up, she might not have felt great, but she was still alive and fighting. Once they put her into that bed, she crumpled like a rag doll. The impression I got was that she felt relieved, in a way, as her whole body seemed to relax and sigh. That made me start wondering how long she had just been holding on? Could it be that she would have passed before this? Even though she stated numerous times that she was ready to go, had she been secretly holding off the inevitable? I will never know.

CHAPTER FOUR

# THE CALL

We got the call in the wee hours Monday morning around 6:00 a.m. I have problems sleeping and did not sleep well that night, having just fallen asleep about two hours before. I had a strong inkling when the phone rang that it was my sister Evelyn about to tell me that mom had passed. I was right. Our mom passed in her sleep and Evelyn had discovered this just before she called. Of all my siblings, I worried about Evelyn the most as she did not think she could handle finding mom dead, but she came through surprisingly well. Although she was crying, she was not hysterical. We told her we would be right over. Although, it is a 20-minute ride to my mom's house, on that morning, it seemed a lot longer. We were the first to arrive, followed by my brother and his wife, then my sister Tina, and then my sister Denise along with her daughter.

Evelyn, after calling us, contacted hospice and they sent a nurse out. As it happens, she was the same nurse who had come by to register mom into the service.

This is the last phase of hospice care. They call the coroner, set the time of death, call the funeral home, and prepare your loved one for the funeral home.

The hospice nurse came in just after my brother arrived and went about preparing my mom for the funeral home. Mom had a catheter inserted so she did not have to worry about getting up to the bathroom.

At the time of death, the body relaxes so all bodily fluids escape and the tongue swells. The nurse took out the catheter, cleaned mom up, and did an excellent job of making her look like she was sleeping. We appreciated her effort and care.

It took the nurse less than an hour to get mom ready. She also contacted the funeral home and the coroner for us, which was very welcome since we did not know how to do this. Of the entire process, I worried the most about contacting the coroner and the police at the time of mom's passing. Hospice took that process out of our hands, and I was very thankful for it.

The nurse asked when we wanted the funeral home to collect mom. Since I was not sure when my sister Denise would arrive, I told her to have them come at 10:00 a.m., thinking Denise should be here before that. Denise was there between 8:00 and 8:30 a.m., so my original thought of 9:00 a.m. would have been fine. Anyway, we had sufficient time with mom to say our goodbyes before the funeral home arrived to collect mom. They moved quickly and placed mom on the gurney and then attempted to move her out the door. However, the gurney was too big to fit through the front door. They ended up having to carry mom out to the gurney they had placed on the porch. They did a fantastic job with compassion and thoughtfulness.

I am thankful that mom had the option to pass at home and that she had the support of all of us, including hospice, to do so. The atmosphere was gentle, quiet, and loving versus the commotion and noise of a hospital.

I have not cried, and I do not think I will. I do not feel sad that mom has passed. Rather, I feel glad that she is no longer in pain and suffering. I felt sad when I became the parent and she became the child in our relationship, and I felt sad when her hands would not stop shaking. I felt sad that her eyes would not focus because of the morphine she took for pain. So, due to the shaking of her hands and unfocused eyes, she could not embroider, which had given her joy and purpose. I felt sad when she could no longer hear and join in conversations with the people who came to visit her or take care of her. However, I do not feel sad that she has passed. Do not confuse my non-sadness with my feeling of loss. Before she died, I had already lost the person I loved who so avidly, sewed and embroidered with, the person with whom I could discuss anything. My mother was my sounding board, and I will miss her greatly.

I wonder if any of you have experienced this feeling of looking out from your body as if you were someone else. I know that I have done this and thought 'Who am I really?' Our perceptions of ourselves are often quite different from how we are perceived by the outside world. For instance, for the past 40 years I have viewed myself as reasonably thin. I was appalled to see myself through the eyes of my grandchildren, who viewed me as overweight. So, now that I am in my 70s, my view of myself has shifted. I have started to experience the limitations of my age through my body, but the view from my mind is different. My mindset is still young, and I am amazed when I do not seem to be able to match my mind view to my physical capabilities.

I share this view of myself to highlight how easy it is to disregard the feelings of our loved ones that we care for that are also going through the same mismatch of mind view and physical limitations. Be kind and thoughtful in your interactions with them as they navigate this rocky path of the aging process.

## The Arrangements

This is the part of the process I was unprepared for, and I hope that I can help any of you reading this to better prepare yourselves when a loved one passes.

You would think that once your loved one passes that now you have all the time in the world or at least a couple of days to process your loss. No, it is one thing right after another.

It started with the funeral home. They called the afternoon mom passed, a Monday. The funeral home would set an appointment for us to make the funeral arrangements. Since this was during COVID, the funeral home told us when we could come.

The funeral home gave us the choice to voice our dislike of the time set for the appointment. We could have stated our preference to wait another day before deciding on the details of the funeral. However, between the urgency, lack of sleep, and numbness we let the funeral home set the pace. Their actions should have felt comforting; instead, it made us angry. A better choice would have been to inform the funeral home of our lack of sleep and to make the appointment for the next day. We did not.

Instead, the funeral home called informing us of the 1:30 p.m. appointment that same day. We had just procured a nice outfit for our mom's viewing and had decided on a lunch location where we could all sit down and get a bite to eat. We would have preferred a sit-down restaurant to help us calm down and give us a rest. However, given the short amount of time (less than an hour): before our funeral home meeting, a fast-food restaurant was our only option.

Our mother had had the foresight to purchase her burial plot and give us instructions on where, how, and what she wanted for her funeral— all except for the last day's tasks. That became our job.

At the funeral home, the director laid our tasks. First, choose a casket, then decide on either a one-day or two-day viewing, next choose the location for the funeral and time, and finally choose a sign-in book and obituary cards before reviewing the funeral contract. It was a lot of information to take in so close to mom's passing and the whole experience had a definite whirlwind feeling. With the funeral arraignments completed, we had one more task to complete: choosing flowers. We agreed to meet at a florist's shop the next day at 10:00 a.m. As my brother was not keen on picking out flowers, we released him from that duty. His wife, Patti happily agreed to go in his stead. With our tasks completed, my siblings and I, exhausted from the day's happenings, returned to our homes.

The next morning, my sisters and sister-in-law and I met at the flower shop. At the florist's, we had to wait to be waited upon, although the full process seemed rushed to me and a little out of balance. I did feel that we might have a tough time agreeing on the arrangements, type of flower, and color, but thankfully we all were able to come to a quick agreement on everything and finished by noon.

Afterward, I thought that did not take long at all. In my heightened emotional state, I had imagined the task as being bigger than it was.

Thankfully, our next task was meeting with the priest who would conduct mom's funeral. That was done on Thursday, which gave us a respite of a day to get back down to earth.

We met with him at 3:00 p.m. My mom made her last day wishes known, including the clothes she wanted to wear, the songs she wanted played, the flowers, viewing and the place of the service. She only got part of her wishes met.

Due to COVID-19 precautions, the funeral home could only manage 25-30 people at a time. Mom's family was large: she had 10 brothers and sisters. We were expecting at least 70 people to come to the funeral, so holding the service at the funeral home was not an option. The church, however, had a vestibule and was large enough to manage the crowd we expected. We chose the vestibule for a one-day viewing. The viewing would commence an hour before the service with the funeral to follow. As this was an unplanned process, we should have expected the unexpected. We found out that another person's funeral was happening at the same time as my mom's funeral, which meant we could not have a procession or grave side service.

She got the clothes, the flowers, the one-day viewing, and the church she wanted. While she did not have her service at the funeral home, they did oversee all the proceedings. However, the church would allow only religious songs, so mom's chosen songs would not be heard. She did not get the procession or a chapel service. She did get the grave side service, just not the scope that she had wanted.

As you plan your own loved one's funeral, just know that sometimes you get Murphy's Law. If the choices you or your loved one had made for what to wear, flowers, service type and length, and place of service do not work out, go with the flow and don't stress over it. It has a way of evening out.

CHAPTER FIVE

# THE FUNERAL

The viewing was set to happen at 10 a.m. and the service to happen at 11 a.m. I was so afraid that I would not wake up in time that I did not sleep well the night before the funeral. However, adrenalin came to my rescue, and I was up at 8:30 a.m., leaving me time enough for a shower and a bit of breakfast.

The vestibule of the church was perfect: spacious, airy, and pleasing to the eye. I do not know if we had 70 attendees, but I do know that we had 60+ people in attendance. Still in the throes of COVID-19, many people were afraid to venture out. Under different circumstances, I am sure we would have more show up.

One hour for the viewing was enough time for people to pay their respects, mingle, and share their memories of our mother. There were no capabilities for a computer slide show, but my sister Tina prepared a lovely picture board of our mom throughout her life. Mom was Catholic, so a mass was held for the service. Near completion of the service, time was given to have people share their memories of mom. I got up and talked about where and when she was born, the places she worked, her marriage and children, and her passions and interests. Also, I shared a couple of stories that happened to her and her brother when they were young. Everyone enjoyed the journey through her life. In addition, my sister Tina authored a poem and a cousin read it aloud to the group.

In a Catholic funeral, there is a procession into the church with the casket and a procession out of the church with the casket, after which the casket is loaded into the hearse to be taken to the cemetery. As there was a conflict with another funeral at the same time as ours, there was no procession to the cemetery or graveside attendance.

From the church we gathered in the church's cafeteria for a meal and remembrance together. Three of my cousins surprised us with a rousing song of *You are My Sunshine*, which was one of my mom's favorite songs. They had sung it with mom on their many visits with her, it seemed fitting to have her walked out of this life with that joyful song.

As I mentioned earlier, things do work out. At the last minute before the funeral, we learned that my siblings could have a graveside service and grave blessing. I was so happy because that graveside blessing was one item that my mom was adamant about wanting and worried wouldn't happen. After everyone left the cafeteria, my husband and I plus our son, my brother and his wife, my niece and her husband, and my nephew and his wife proceeded to the gravesite. Lucky for us the priest agreed to do a gravesite blessing. It was quick, sweet and to the point, so it did not take much time. By this time, my energy rapidly started flagging. I had not realized how tightly I was holding myself. It was apparent when we arrived home and I sat in my chair as I fell asleep almost immediately. I do not sleep well at night and usually don't take naps during the day because of my insomnia. However, I did not have any problem sleeping that night and it actually refreshed me.

I was numb for the first couple of weeks after the funeral. Not only was I feeling the loss of my mom, but I was also missing the structure and purpose of going out to her house twice a week. Part of me was rejoicing that I did not have that task anymore while the other part of me missed it greatly. I was thinking "Now what do I do with myself?"

I am sure this is the classic example of the hole that one feels when a loved one passes, especially if you were remarkably close and dealt daily with his/her health care. This care consumed so much of your daily life that it has become woven into your life. Now that you no longer have that care to perform, it creates a hole in your routine. Fortunately for me, I have many projects before me to do, so it did not take long for that hole to be filled up. However, I know that for many people they find it harder to replace that time with other projects or passions and to fill the hole left in their heart.

May I suggest that first be kind to yourself, give yourself the gift of mourning. Only return to a busier schedule when you feel ready. When you are ready, discover the pursuits that give you joy and pursue them. If there are pursuits you have wanted to explore but felt you did not have the time to do so, now is the time to explore them. Then just focus on the enjoyment of doing that passion. It might feel wooden to participate at first, but as you proceed, I feel you will slowly close the hole with other more enjoyable pursuits.

Please do not feel guilty for doing so, as your loved one would not have wanted you to be unhappy or unable to move forward in your life. He/she would have wanted you to be happy, fulfilled, and full of passion for the things in life.

I know my mom would not have wanted me or my siblings to mourn her forever but rather to remember her and her teachings and to find joy and purpose in our lives once again. And foremost, she would have wanted all of us to be happy.

# CHAPTER SIX

# THE EPIPHANY

Mom was diagnosed with cancer in the spring of 2018 and given six months to live. Here we were going into 2021 and I started to question when she would pass.

It is not possible to live like that day in and day out, like waiting for the shoe to drop, you cannot keep it up. In the last few months before mom passed, we had to increase the frequency of our visits with her. My brother and I started coming twice a week. And during her last few weeks, it was "All Hands-on Deck" with daily visits for all of us.

I remember coming home from a particularly tough day when mom was especially obstinate about whatever we were trying to do for her that day. I pulled into my driveway, turned off the truck, and just sat there for a few minutes leaning back in my seat with my head against the headrest. I let out a sigh as my gaze went to the sky. I was struck by how the sky felt expansive and peaceful yet how small I was in comparison. It struck me oddly that I felt this feeling and I wondered what it meant. Then the epiphany hit me. Since the day I had found out my mother's days were numbered, I gradually diminished, day by day, becoming more compact/emotionally shut down to get through this period. I realized that I could no longer diminish myself any further. The expansiveness of the sky highlighted for me my feeling of smallness. Also, I could no longer hide from the feelings that came with the eventuality of my mother's passing. I had to open and face those feelings and go through the pain of her loss.

At that moment, I made up my mind to embrace all the essences of my mother and enjoy the time we had left. We enjoyed talking about embroidery, particularly hand embroidery, and I discovered machine embroidery during this time too. She would light up if asked what project she was working on at the time. And she would regale listeners with how she picked the colors and design for pieces she worked on. This kind of conversation I will miss.

When I think of our family and the losses we have sustained over the past few years, our family's fabric is indeed a bit tattered. My mom was number seven of 11 children, and now her youngest sister is the only one remaining. I know losses are inevitable and so we are conditioned for that to happen. What we are not prepared for is the hole in our reality that the people we lose leave in our hearts and lives. Along with the ache of lost love and missing that persons' essence, the void their absence leaves in our lives is the hardest to deal with as we try to move on with our own lives.

I was reflecting upon my mother's last couple of years and what she went through. She not only was fighting the effects of cancer, plus feeling extremely cold and unable to get warm all the time, but she also had cellulitis that left her legs raw, weeping, and peeling. Except for the last couple of months of her life, through it all she kept her humor and her love of life. I now think that I started to mourn the loss of my mother— the person she was, not the vessel she became at the end— when we met at the oncologist's office in June of 2018, and he outlined my mother's treatment options and she chose not to do any of them. I steeled myself for the eventuality of her passing. As she went through the process of gradual dying, it was like a roller coaster ride. At first, she had very few bad days. Later, she would get sick, and we thought this is it but then she would snap out it. By the time we reached June 2020, the roller coaster ride was starting to wear on me, my four siblings, and my mother as well. To help our sister who lived with our mom, my brother and I increased our visits/lunch days from once to twice a week, spending a few hours on those days. It became increasingly hard to find food that mom wanted or that her stomach would accept. For a person who made everything from scratch, and very nutritious I might add, she had a tough time accepting anything less. Feeding her was a nightmare for my sister who lived with her. After a particularly distressing day during which mom would not accept any food and her mood was spiraling down, I felt so sad at her pain and so frustrated that I could not do anything about it. I am also going to admit that my strongest feeling at that point was "When will this end?" I felt so guilty afterward for feeling this. It meant I also wanted my mother to pass so I would not feel bad any longer. If you are also going through something similar dear reader, it is natural. We are only human, and we will feel like this from time to time. It is part of our natural self-preservation to protect ourselves above all others. However, as a society we have exalted the mindset to not think in this way. Once I brought this feeling out in the open, I felt better and, in a way, it gave me strength to face the reality before me. In that instant I knew I had started to mourn the person she was, my loving mother, teacher, comrade in sewing/embroidery arts, and wise counsel. Being the eldest, I was fortunate to have known her in all the phases a parent can be, as a life giver, nurturer, mentor, teacher, counselor, and finally I could see her as a person who was a woman with all the wants, feelings, and desires that I had as a person. So, instead of just my mother, I saw her as a person/woman who was my equal.

There were many times in the last couple of months of her life when mom's armor started to shine less, when she was doing things that showed me the person, not my mother. For example, when I was young if we had refused to eat the food placed before us because it tasted bad or we didn't like it for some reason, we would get the lecture about people starving in other parts of the world so we should highly value what we had in front of us. It amused and appalled me that she had become just an ordinary person and had started to waste food unabashedly and apparently without any remorse, forgetting about all those starving people.

Hence, I was saddened by the passing of my mother, but I could not cry for the person who passed. My mother lives within me, she has imbued herself into me, she is the voice of my conscience, she is the muse of my creations, so I have lost nothing and there is no need for tears.

In contrast to my mother's passing, which was expected, the passing of my sister's son and later her husband were both unexpected and brought many tears. This is partly because I recognized the depth of pain my sister was feeling and partly because I mourn the unique people her husband and son were, and I miss both dearly. It's hard enough to lose a child, but when he or she is your only child, the pain is doubly hard— particularly since her son required a closed-casket funeral. To say the least, many life highlights, my sister would never go through with the loss of her son. I was devastated at my sister's loss, which reminded me of my own two children and how I would cope if either of them had passed. However, life was not done with her, as she lost our mother and then her husband within 10 days of each other. I give my sister credit for her strength as she withstood that devastating loss of all the people, she held most dear in her life.

Today I was thinking about my sister Tina and wondering how she was feeling as she returned to work. I imagined her co-workers coming up to her to offer condolences for the loss of both her mom and her husband. I thought about how she and the rest of the family will have to deal with these losses going forward. It feels as if the very fabric of our family has been punctured, the woven fibers torn, and holes formed.

Because my other siblings and I had to take care of my mother's property and belongings, we could not help her with her husband's. Thankfully, she and her husband had many friends who stepped in and helped her out. They reroofed her garage, helped clean out and sell all the toys that her husband had collected, and then they helped move her when she sold her house and gave her a place to stay while she looked for another smaller place to live. I don't really understand how she is managing all the loss that has come into her life. I have not really asked her but do see that she is managing it reasonably well. Despite all the losses she suffered, Tina told me and our other siblings that she felt guilty for not helping with our mother's things, never once complaining about all she was going through. This is a testament to her type and strength of character.

What I am trying to say here is that death and mourning are highly personal and selective feelings that are unique to each person. From my personal experience, the level of closeness affected my feelings of loss. My nephew Jesse, my dad, my aunts and uncles, my animals, all those losses affected me differently each time and were unique to each person and how I knew them. Mostly my sadness was directed to the people closest to the loved one who passed as I saw how their loss affected those left behind.

For my readers who need the closeness and compassion of like-feeling people during their own challenging experiences, I can recommend the many compassionate, helpful, and wonderful bereavement groups out there waiting to help you through your time of loss. Initially you may not want or need the support, but down the road, when all others have moved on and you are alone with your grief, there is support available for you. Contact hospice in your area, run a web search for grief support groups or your community's outreach services.

Structure will also be important during your time of mourning. After some time of personal mourning, it could be good for you to attend a grief support group—not only to help support others who are experiencing feelings of loss but for the simple reason of getting you out of your house. I know that joining a group is probably the last thing you would want to do at such a time but consider for a moment the value of losing yourself in an activity that you want to do. Maybe you won't feel this right away, but as you engage in this chosen activity week after week, it will help diminish the pain of your loss. Eventually, your loss will soften into remembrance instead of mourning, especially with the help of fellow sufferers.

CHAPTER SEVEN

# AFTERMATH AND MOVING FORWARD

After the funeral, my siblings and I discussed what to do with our mom's house and the contents that remained. An end-of-September date was initially chosen to begin the cleanup. However, my brother got anxious and couldn't wait, so we dove in and got started sometime around the middle of September.

We rented a dumpster to help get rid of all the unnecessary items that we knew would not sell or could not be donated. After 65 years of residing in the same house, treasures filled her home. She was an avid cook, sewer, DIY enthusiast, and a garage sale, Goodwill, St. Paul DeVincent attendee. Hence, her house was filled with art paints, fabric, sewing machines, picture frames, and all things creative. She did not buy junk, but chose wisely when purchasing any items, and she kept them in decent shape despite the years of use. On the other hand, she did not throw out anything that she felt was still useful and those were the items for which we needed the dumpster. We took three full truckloads of items to a resale shop, threw out a ton of items, and we still had more to remove at the end of a week of cleaning and packing.

It took three more all-day cleaning sessions to finally get rid of everything. Two of my siblings and I had mature homes of our own that were already full to the brim. Our two remaining siblings were house hunting, so a lot of items that might have gone home with them had to be donated. And we had to be mindful of items that belonged to our sister Evelyn who was still living in the house.

Once the house was clean, we tackled the kitchen's problem of outdated cabinetry. Lucky for us, my brother was able to make new cabinet doors and, with the help of his wife, Patti, painted the existing cabinets, which made the whole kitchen bright and updated. Once cabinets were painted, we contacted a realtor to place the house on the market.

One challenge we faced when showing the house was that our sister Evelyn, who had been living with our mom, was also working from home at that point due to COVID-19. Fortunately, her job allowed her leeway in her work schedule. Initially she was able to leave when prospects came by for a showing. However, as the house showings became more frequent, we agreed to let her decide whether or not to accept an appointment to make showings more convenient with her work schedule.

We were listing the house as an "AS IS" sale. We knew the roof needed replacement. We fixed all the smaller things, like updating the kitchen, and we cleaned the house well. We received three offers and chose what we felt at the time was the best offer. During the buyer's inspection process, they found mold in the attic. This prompted them to adjust their initial offer, reducing our asking price by a total of $27,500, which was unacceptable. At that point, my siblings and I decided to have a professional fix the mold problem and have the roof redone. We then would place the house back on the market at a higher price and see what happens. If we had done what I have suggested to you readers, we would have had our mom's house sold twice, as we had two solid offers, with the last one ready to buy.

Should you have to face the liquidation of belongings and the sale of your loved one's property, to save yourself time, money, and frustration, I pass on the following suggestions:

1. ***Hire someone to do a deep clean of your loved one's house or do it yourself.***

   If your loved one has been in their house for a long time, there are places that just have not seen a good clean in long time. It is not a reflection of whether they are good housekeepers or not, it is just small, out of traffic areas in a house that do not see movement and attract dust and dirt.

2. ***Reduction of household items.***

   If you can at all start a reduction of your loved one's unnecessary items, have a list of takers for these treasured pieces before they pass on. This will not be an easy task, especially if your loved one has extreme attachment to some items. That is okay, do what you can.

3. ***Home Inspection.***

   Have a home inspection done by a reputable inspector, who will list problems, code violations, and any cosmetic problems that need addressing before you place the house on the market. Addressing these issues ahead of time will help the sale of the house go more smoothly, will help ensure money spent on repairs will have a better chance of being recouped, and will draw a higher price for the house overall.

4. ***Appraisal of House and Property***

   This option will need the consent of your loved one before it can be initiated. In our case, since our mother was in her residence for 65 years, we had no way of knowing what her house was worth. We thought it prudent, and our mother agreed, to find out the house's value. In our case, I was friends with a realtor, and he gave me a realtor's assessment about 11 years prior to my mom's passing. This gave us a benchmark to go by at the time of her passing. We could have hired a professional assessor but at the time we had no plans to sell, so a more in-depth estimate was not needed.

5. ***Assigning of a Trustee and POA (Power of Attorney)***

I am very thankful to my parents who in 1974 decided to initiate a Living Trust for their assets, funeral wishes, and all the things that go with that process. As I was the eldest child, they named me trustee of the will and their medical advocate. If I could not fulfill my duties, my brother was listed as second trustee. My dad passed away in 1998 when he was 79 and my mom was 72, so the living will did not come into play, as my mother inherited everything as the surviving spouse. It was when she reached her eighties and almost passed away due to a bowl resection operation, and became infected with Mercer Staph that I took the initiative to find out what my duties entailed. As a medical advocate, I learned that I was responsible for making decisions regarding medical procedures and treatments if my mother was unable to do that herself. As her POA, I was also responsible for managing her financial affairs. And finally, I was responsible for managing her funeral arraignments and the liquidation and sale of her estate after she passed.

The first thing I did was get my mother to agree to place the house and land in the trust's name. I did this to protect her assets while she lived and to make it easier to sell her house after she passed. With the house and land in the trust's name, I as trustee I had full rights to sell and distribute any of her final assets. I placed a copy of the updated court records regarding the deed to the property and house in the living will.

The second thing I put into motion was I had my mother determine what items she wanted to pass on and to whom. I listed them and had each of my siblings' sign and date beside the item they were to inherit and then had my mother sign and date the full document. I placed that document into the living will for future use. In the end this action was unnecessary for us since most of the items my mother wanted to pass on, she gave to each person before she passed. and the remaining items were no longer wanted at the time of her passing. However, I felt that taking this step did prevent any hard feelings, knowing our mother's wishes were fulfilled.

The fourth thing I did was request permission from my mom to have a lawyer look over the trust. Since the trust had been initiated in 1974, having a lawyer go over the trust to make sure everything was up to date seemed like a solid idea. I do not know the initial cost for creating the living will, but the update cost $150, which I felt was money well spent. The lawyer deemed the trust in good working order and only had to update the HIPPA agreement.

The fifth thing I did was to get our mother to okay having my sister, brother, and myself be co-signers on her checking and savings accounts. In simpler times, it was easier to manage a loved one's estate; however, in our more complex modern times, if you are not a signee on an account, you are unable to access or even receive information regarding that account. I did not want that to be a problem, so I asked mom if my sister, brother, and I could be signers on her checking/saving account. My mom agreed that it would be a responsible idea to put us on her account and she gave us permission to receive debit cards for that account. The reasoning was that my sister who lived with my mom paid all her bills, and my brother would need access after she passed to purchase anything needed to fix up her house up, and I needed to manage any other bills and to distribute her estate.

The sixth thing I did was to have a signature stamp made up with my mom's name when she was still able to sign her name well. As time passed, my mom was fortunate that she could still sign her name even if it took a bit longer for her to do so. In retrospect, I wish I had insisted she used the stamp during her illness, since she had to sign so many documents.

The last thing I helped my mother do, through her banking institution, was to set up a trust account in the living will trust's name for her IRA funds and her yearly distribution to go into. In this type of account, my mom was the sole signature signer. As her POA, I could view the account, but I could not access any funds unless I had the permission of my mother. After she passed, the POA ceased but then I became the trustee with full rights to the account. With the checking account in the trust's name, and the checking account in my mom's name, I had two accounts where I could cash any checks/funds that came in after my mother's passing. My mother was a stickler for paying bills a year at a time if she could. Just before her passing, she paid her house insurance for the year on the first of August. She passed 16 days later. Once the house was sold, we would receive a rebate from the insurance company. Having these accounts ready made it easy and efficient to deposit funds from the sale of the house and her tax refund and to take care of the final transactions and disbursements.

I am so glad that I had the foresight to implement these changes to the living will when I did. It proved beneficial when she did pass, as it made it so simple to take care of fixing and preparing the house for sale, paying outstanding bills, and handling the final incoming monies from the sale of the house. All transactions went smoothly.

If the above suggestions can be achieved and implemented, you will have less to do at the time of your loved one's passing.

CHAPTER EIGHT

# THE STAGES OF GRIEF

The process of a loved one's passing is difficult at best but due to well-meaning friends, acquaintances, and others, it can be an ongoing test of protecting your tender feelings. Although they mean well with their words of encouragement and urges to do this and that to get on with your life, never feel that you need to rush the grieving process. It is solely up to you how you go through the grieving of a loved one. Like anything that we do in our lives, we must crawl before we walk. If we did not do that process correctly, then we would eventually have to repeat it until we got it right. Therefore, going through the five stages of grief is important. They are defined as:

- Denial
- Anger
- Bargaining
- Depression
- Acceptance

When reviewing the above stages, I found that they did not accurately describe my personal grief process which I can share with you what I did to go through with the loss of my mother.

- *Remembrance*— I immersed myself in remembering who my mother was to me, the good and the bad. I thought about all she gave me and did for me in her life. Also, I thought about her life in general, honoring her journey. Then I did one thing for myself, I immersed myself in my machine embroidery. I had started during my mom's illness but had felt so distracted with all that was happening that I could not delve deep enough into it to retain the knowledge I needed.

Immerse yourself in their memory but also do something each day for yourself. It can be as simple as going for coffee at a place you consider special or comfy. Read a favorite book. The goal is to shift your focus from your loved one's life to your life. This does not imply in any way that you forget them but simply that you make it easier for you to go on with your life. I found that the more I did for myself, the less pain I felt from the loss of my mother. You might find yourself doing a yearly personal memorial of your loved one's passing. My sister, who lost her son when he was eighteen to a car crash would every year on the anniversary of his passing, she requests we not contact her because she would be morning her son at that time. This process is a very personal one and how acute your bond with your loved was will reflect how deeply this memorial will play out in your life.

- *Expressing your feelings*— It is particularly important, I feel, to find someone you can talk to about how you feel regarding the loss of a loved one. Expressing those feelings to a trusted person will help diminish your pain, or at least the intensity of those feelings. If you are angry, get a sturdy pillow that you either can punch or beat against the wall to help you release the anger within you. Cry, yell if you need to do so, and release that pent up energy. At first you will be highly emotional, so you will need a friend that has big shoulders. If you do not have such a friend, then there are many excellent grief groups. In them you will meet others who are going through the same process as you and will have the understanding and compassion you need to help you heal from this loss. As you heal, you will also help others just by coming to group meetings to share your experiences and. To access this type of resource, either call your local health department or search the web for grief groups near you, I am sure you will find excellent groups that can help you.

- *Take your time*— No one has the right to tell you that it's time to move on until you are ready to do so. Grief is very personal; you will know when you have reached a crossroads and are ready to move forward with your life. It has been 10 months since my mother's passing, and I am now able to resume doing my favorite things. I was depressed and did not know it, I just felt extremely tired and none of my usual passions seemed imperative for me to do. You may not recognize that you are going through this fog of grief until you look back and see plainly that it happened to you.

I am as guilty of this as the next person. I have told my sister numerous times what I thought she should do, thinking that would help her and be supportive. However, all it did was make her sadder. I later learned that it made her feel guilty after a while to be still in the mourning process. I did not understand that a hole had been created in her life with the loss of her son. At best, the pain would diminish more like a scar that would not heal. At any time, the scab could tear off and the pain revisited. I feel badly that I contributed to her pain with my lack of understanding about what she was experiencing. Now I am more aware and if talks about her son, I listen and speak with her about him. It is the least I can do for her.

- *Refocus*— Once the pain and the fog have diminished and you can again entertain the idea of rejoining the world, find a passion that excites you and focus on it. At first, it will seem hard, and you will not put your full heart into it. However, gradually it will fill you and it will be easier to do. If you are unable to get into a project by yourself, join a group that promotes that passion. The group might have small projects to do that will help get you started. At the least they will help get you talking about it. And the best part is that you will have like minds to discuss your passion and bounce ideas off.

For myself, I only focused on a small part of a project and did not beat myself up if I did not do more on the project. At first, I did not find joy in doing it, but gradually my interest and desire returned. I was not affected by the loss of my mother as much as my two younger sisters or my brother were. The effects of loss probably impacted them differently and more acutely than me, but I still found it hard do anything that I previously had found fun to do.

- ***Avoid Big Decisions***— Due to your extreme mental state at a time of grief, it is unwise to make any kind of big decisions. The funeral process is taxing enough decision-, so try to hold off in making decisions about moving, selling your house, or buying a subscription. The bottom line here is that you will not make wise choices due to the blinders put on you by grief. You have time to make those decisions when the brain fog passes, and you once again can think clearly. I have no period of time or magic number for this to happen. I have heard suggestions to wait for at least six months. Sometimes, we do not have the luxury of time, and many decisions need to be made at times like these. If that is the case in your life, please reach out to someone you trust to help you to make those decisions. For one thing, they can help you make quick decisive decisions and another they will have a clearer view of the situation at hand.

The loss of a loved one is the most emotional time in our lives, and we will feel many different emotions— often many at same time. It is okay to feel glad that a loved one passed, especially if they were experiencing extreme pain or were uncomfortable or unhappy. You are human and you will feel relief, along with anger, sadness, abandonment, and depression. These are all normal feelings of a human being, and they will pass. In time, you will regain balance in your emotions, your life, and you will return to happiness, although you may feel your loss for an extended time.

I decided to use my web browser to find how many grief counselor or centers were near my zip code, and several popped up with a map showing where they were in relationship to my house, plus a telephone number and address.

Another thing I did is ask my siblings for their thoughts regarding our mother's passing, long-term care, hospice, her cancer, her funeral, and the disbursement of her estate. This is what they shared with me in their own words.

1. **What was your reaction to the news our mom had cancer and your observations on how mom handled it?**
- Denise— It did not surprise me, as mom had been ill for numerous years. However, I was very upset thinking that she would be in pain and suffer a great deal. I never wanted mom to go through any of this, as she was unhappy most of her life and she did not deserve additional trauma. I believe mom handled the news as most individuals would: she denied it at the beginning, then moved to wanting to cure this disease, then she accepted it.
- Tina— It was devastating for me, and I think mom was scared.
- Evelyn—With mom already having had cancer two previous times and surgery, she seemed to take it with a grain of salt. She already had made funnies about having so much done to her and so many items removed from her.

- RJ— My reaction: not much I could do about it. Mom's reaction: the cancer itself— not much more that she could not get out like she used to.

2. **What were your personal thoughts regarding death and about mom's pending demise from cancer or old age?**

- Denise— This may sound cold and uncaring; however, I accepted the information as it is all part of life. With mom in her later years, it was easier for me. I only wish she would have forgiven the people who wronged her. I know this is more for me in knowing our Lord Jesus would take her in his arms. I only pray that Jesus forgave her and comforted her.
- Tina— (No response...)
- Evelyn— I hated seeing my mom change over the year with everything she had gone through and had put up with over the years. She worked so hard to have everything she had. She devoted her life to her family.
- RJ— I believe there are four types of death: expected, unexpected, wanted, and unwanted. My mother wanted to die and was tired of living with the lack of movement.

3. **What were your observations and thoughts regarding the care hospice gave to mom?**

- Denise— This one is difficult for me to answer as I was only at the house twice when they came by. I just know that mom appreciated the ladies and felt that they were her friends.
- Tina— I really cannot answer this one as I wasn't a part of a lot of it. I heard hearsay and just know at one point when her legs were really bad, hospice didn't take care of her properly. They did not contact us to talk to us about mom's end of life. I thought that was not as good as care like the days before her passing.
- Evelyn— Hospice was a Godsend. All the nurses that came to check on mom were angels.
- RJ— They were good, caring people.

4. **In what areas do you feel hospice could have done better, or were they okay?**

- Denise— As far as I know, they handled things very well.

- Tina— I feel that hospice could have done a better job taking care of mom.
- Eve— In my opinion, hospice went over and above in taking care of my mom.
- RJ— I thought their care was okay.

5. **What were your feelings, thoughts, and observations regarding mom's declining health from the time we found out she had cancer until her death?**

- Denise— I was very happy that we had mom much longer than the doctors informed us. I am also very happy that she wasn't in a lot of pain until her last few days. Or, (if she was), she was good at covering up the pain.
- Tina— It was devasting to see her decline every time I came in and took care of her, to see the differences in her and how much she was in pain and was uncomfortable, that was very hard to see. I feel mom did not deserve the way she went on to her eternal life.
- Evelyn— Each day she would change. It started with not wanting to sleep in her bed and instead sleeping in her recliner, yet she would not put her legs up. Her legs were retaining water more and more. Her appetite was getting worse, and she slept more and more.
- RJ— My mother wanted to die and was tired of living with the lack of movement.

6. **What are your personal views on death?**

- Denise— Death does not frighten me as I look forward to seeing Our Lord Jesus. However, I am afraid of any pain that may be associated with death. I only pray that Our Lord Jesus would comfort me during that time.
- Tina— Death is hard, the loss of somebody that you cared for in love knowing that you are not going to ever see them again. You feel empty, lost, and all those memories and what you have every single day you are never going to have again. It hurts your gut and aches every day. You cry, you get mad, you want to throw fits, and you want to scream to the top of your lungs.

You do not want to eat and do not want to do anything or go anywhere. Even though people want you to go, you do not want to go. You get to the point where you just do not care. You try to move on, but you do not want to forget them or what they looked like, and the hardest thing is not having them anymore and you have to move on with your life without them.

- Evelyn— It was the hardest thing I have ever been through, and I still have images of finding my mom (after she passed). I wished I would have stayed downstairs to be with her when she passed. She passed away all by herself and I regret not being there for her. I wished that more of my siblings would have stayed with me and mom. I knew once she was placed in the bed, she would not last.

- RJ— I believe there are four types of death: expected, unexpected, wanted and unwanted.

7. **What were your observations and views of the funeral process and the funeral itself?**

- Denise— I know that my older sister took care of most of the funeral process and I truly appreciated it. She also included all the siblings in the decisions involving the funeral.

- Tina— I was not able to participate or observe any of mom's process of the funeral or visitations due to dealing with my husband's illness at the time.

- Evelyn— With everything going on with the virus and losing another family member, mom desired a better funeral than she was given.

- RJ— The viewing, service, and funeral went well.

8. **What were your observations and views of getting the house ready for sale and removal and disbursal of mom's things?**

- Denise— I believe mom did an excellent job of "cleaning house" before she passed. She ensured that everything was given away or marked for the individuals she wished to have her things. The largest issue was getting mom to dispose of all the other items she had. She had a very hard time letting go of the things she worked so hard to obtain. I was very impressed with all of my siblings that they were always there to help with all that was involved even though it took weeks to complete it all.

- Tina— I really did not take part in helping in the process of the removal or getting ready for the process of selling mom's house. I had a small part in it. It was hard and devastating to think that how a woman or a couple had their memories in this house... and to think my house that I grew up in we were selling. It was very devastating. (Tina's husband passed at the same time, so she was dealing with the same process with her own house.)

- Evelyn— Since I lived with my mom, I felt I was rushed to move out. Sending me out of town to be able to fix up the kitchen and coming home to a big mess was not fun. When I left the house, almost all the clutter was going, no more piles to look at. I lived there for so many years and now was homeless. Getting rid of mom's things went well.

- RJ— It should have been more organized, with more delegation of duties, and more communication and labeling of what belongs to whom.

9. **What would have been done differently in readying the house for sale or distribution of mom's things?**

- Denise— I can't think of anything because if we had tried to begin the process sooner, it would have made mom think that we were ready to get rid of her and her things. I think we have done well on what we did by dividing up everything that we all wanted. I think mom did a very fine job of preparing us, by gathering us all together for meetings and having us write down what we wanted and documenting it. I think that is the best thing to have a family do is to gather, have meetings, and have the chance to agree or disagree. This way everybody can have their opinion known or make their opinions known.

- Tina— I really did not take part in helping in the process of the removal or getting ready for the process of selling mom's house, although I did take a small part in it. It was hard and devastating to think how a woman or couple had their memories in this house…and to think my house that I grew up in was going to be sold. This was completely devastating for me.

- Evelyn— (No comment.)
- RJ— It should have been more organized, with more delegation of duties, and more communication and labeling of what belongs to whom.

10. **What were your observations, views, thoughts on the sale of the house process?**

- Denise— I believe it worked out well. Everyone was involved and everything was done with everyone's approval.
- Tina— I can't answer this one. I was not involved with a lot of the process of the sale of the house. Although, I think it went smooth and I think the decisions that we all made by gathering and making all the decisions together were the best. I think our realtor did a very fine job of informing us on the process and with the buyers and information that we needed.
- Evelyn— (No comment.)
- RJ— All went well, and my siblings were in total agreement.

11. **Do you have any insights/views of what one can do to ready their loved ones for their declining years?**

- Denise— Try to put yourself in your loved one's shoes. Ask yourself How would I feel if I were asked to give, throw, or donate items that I owned or worked hard to have?" Keep your parents' feelings at the forefront as it is their last days of their lives. Make them as happy as possible before they are gone.
- Tina— To have in place a will, living will, a trust, set beneficiaries, appointed executors, appoint power attorneys to their estate. Also, have bank accounts to set executors and beneficiaries and have additional names on the accounts.
- Evelyn— If there is a sibling in the family, they need to help more and not just go on with their life and step up for the family member that is taking care of the mother or father.
- RJ— Do what you can to make them happy and comfortable.

# CHAPTER NINE

# WILL VS. LIVING WILL VS. DOING NOTHING AND PAYING TAXES

After my mom nearly passed in her 80's it became apparent that someone should be reading the Living Trust agreement to find out what the necessary steps were if she passed. It was at that time that I took the initiative in taking the necessary steps to perform my duties. In Chapter Seven I listed the actions I took and gave full details of how I implemented them. I feel they are important enough to touch on them in this section again.

- **Obtaining a Living Will, Will and assigning a Power of Attorney**

  I was thankful that my parents had foresight to implement a Living Will Trust in 1974 and make me and my brother trustees.

  In these times it is important to have measures in place to protect yourself and your assets if you or your spouse suddenly passes. If you have everything set up in your accounts that has your spouse's name on them or as a beneficiary, those assets will be passed to him/her. But if you have nothing in place, then that can be a problem for your loved one who remains. Probate is costly in time and in money and painful for your loved ones. A simple will can protect you to a certain degree, but it can be contested.

The best protection for your property and assets is a living will in conjunction with a last will and testament. A living will is a directive pertaining to your wishes regarding your medical treatment and your wishes regarding resuscitation and extension of your life. A last will and testament lay out all your assets, your wishes regarding them, how they are to be distributed, and who will preside over that distribution after you pass.

- **Adding trusted signers or beneficiaries to financial accounts**

  I was relieved that my mom agreed and thought it was a good idea to add myself, my brother and my sister who lived with her to her checking account. Also, it prevented hard feelings between my siblings, knowing this was our mother's wishes.

  I am so glad that I had the foresight to implement the changes to the living will when I did. It proved beneficial when she did pass as it made it so simple to take care of the fixing/preparing the house for sale, paying outstanding bills, and depositing and then disbursing the final incoming monies received from the sale of the house. All went smoothly. One thing that I was cautioned against doing was placing any of our mother's assets in any one of our names, due to the possibility that if a lawsuit was even brought against mom or any one of us, then our own assets could be taken along with hers. A living will can offer more security against this possibility.

- **Updating of financial records, deeds, Living Wills, Wills, or any documents related to your estate.**

  My mother's Living Will was drawn up in 1974, so it made good sense to have it looked over by an attorney. All was in order except the HIPPA (Health Insurance Portability and Accountability Act)

- **Assets Assessed, Transferring/Assigning of Assets**

  A fair market assessment of a home and property fee is between $280-$330 in Michigan.

  My parents built their house and owned the land since 1953. Hence, we had no idea how much it was worth. My mother did not want to sell the house but did want to know how much it was worth. I decided to call a friend who was a real estate agent who gave us a fair-market value appraisal and did not charge for this service. My friend cautioned us that it would not be a true assessment but a ballpark figure to work from when eventually decided to sell.

- **Determining Taxes, Income Tax, Inheritance Tax, Etc.**

  Per taxes, since every state has different laws in place regarding, death, inheritance, and state taxes, I suggest asking your state authority regarding your options for these procedures/policies.

  For our state, we do not have a death tax, nor is there a state tax assessed. Our inheritance tax states that if your loved one's assets are below $250,000, you do not have to pay anything. And since my mother never sold her house before this, we were able to claim the credit for senior selling their house. (Per https://www. investopedia.com/terms/t/taxpayer-relief-act-of-1997. asp, a 1997 act exempts taxation on capital gains on the sale of a personal residence worth up to $500,000 for married couples who file taxes jointly and $250,000 for single individuals and that the taxpayer (s) have occupied in at least two of the last five years. The exemption can only be claimed once every two years.)

We were able to sell the house shortly after mom passed and we did not accrue any capital gains above the allowed amount. The only thing that she received was a state homestead refund for energy usage. Mom didn't earn enough on Social Security to pay any Federal Tax or interest on her bank accounts which needed to be above $600 in our state.

- **Death Certificates**

  Another item that we could have been prepared for was death certificates. How many are really needed?

  If your loved one had outstanding loans, bank accounts, credit cards and/or IRAs, you might have to have a certified copy (state seal on the document) for each of these entities.

  My mother had no credit cards, house payment, or loans so we did not need copies for them. She did have a money market account and a checking account, plus house insurance and the sale of her house. Only two creditors required hard copies of the death certificate house insurance and the sale of her house. The bank took the original and made a digital copy for their files. Since we live in a digital age, you might find that most entities will accept a digital copy in lieu of a hard copy.

## More on Living Wills, Trusts, & the Like

The links below represent a small sampling of all the information available about living wills and trusts and are supplied as a way to get you started in your own research.

1. Inheritance Tax: What It Is, How It's Calculated, and Who Pays It: https://www.investopedia.com › terms › inheritance tax

2. Tax-Efficient Wealth Transfer – Investopedia: https://www. investopedia.com › articles › reduce-estate-tax

3. The Benefits and Shortcomings of a Revocable Trust: https://www. fiduciarytrust.com › trust-estate--tax-planning

4. Revocable trust vs. irrevocable trust: Key differences ... – FreeWill: https://www.freewill.com › learn › revocable-trust-vs-irre...

5. Drawbacks of a Living Trust – Nolo: https://www.nolo.com › technical-support-main › nolo-liv...

6. Do Living Trusts Protect Assets from Creditors? – LegalZoom: https://www.legalzoom.com › articles › do-living-trusts-pr...

7. Abusive Trust Tax Evasion Schemes - Questions and Answers – IRS: https://www.irs.gov › small-businesses-self-employed › ab...

8. Benefits of a Living Trust vs. a Will | Fort Mill SC | Cornelius NC: https://www.nosaljeterlaw.com › benefits-living-trust-vs-will

9. Who Are Death Certificates Given To? What Officials Require Them? https://www.neptunesociety.com › ask-a-funeral-director and Who needs death certificates when someone dies?

10. Is Probate Required if There is a Will? - Morrish Solicitors: https:// www.morrishsolicitors.com › is-probate-required-if... and Who decides if probate is needed?

11. Inheretance Law Pertraining to FirstBorn or Oldest Children

legalbeagle.com/12722265-inheritance-laws-pertaining-to-first-born-or-oldest-children.html

12. What Happens to a Bank Account When Someone Dies? - The Balance .//www.thebalancemoney.com › what-happens-to-a-b

CHAPTER TEN

# Is Hospice Right for You, Your Loved One, and Your Family?

Once you loved has been referred by a doctor into Hospice care. Deciding whether or not to enroll your loved one in hospice care is a deeply personal and complex decision to make. When searching for information about hospice care, the following resources were helpful to me.

1.	Hospice care: Comforting the terminally ill - Mayo Clinic: https://www.mayoclinic.org › hospice-care › art-20048050

2.	Medicare Hospice Benefit Game Answer Explanations: https://pogoe.org › sites › default › files

3.	Refusing Hospice Care: Examining a Patient's Rights and Responsibilities:  https://pathwayshealth.org › hospice-topics › refusing-hos

4.	The Admission Process | Hospice & Palliative Care:  https://hospicecareinc.org › the-admission-process

5.	How and Where Is Hospice Care Provided and How Is It Paid For? https://www.cancer.org › who-provides-hospice-care

6.      Assessment Tools for Palliative Care:  https://effectivehealthcare.ahrq.gov › research-protocol

7.      Does Hospice Stay Overnight [2021]:  https://hospicevalley.com › does-hospice-stay-overnight

8.      The Plan Of Care - CompassionCare Hospice:  https://compassioncarenevada.com › hospice-care-the-pla.

9.      Frequently Asked Questions | BJC Hospice:  https://www.bjchospice.org › About-Us › FAQ

10.     Clinical Intentions of Antibiotics Prescribed to Patients on Discharge:  https://www.ncbi.nlm.nih.gov › articles › PMC5849491

11.     What Hospice Does and Doesn't Do - Next Avenue:  https://www.nextavenue.org › what-hospice-does-and-doe

12.     How is Hospice Covered? https://www.skirballhospice.org › services › costs

13.     Simply Money: Can Medicare take you home to pay for hospice? https://www.fox19.com › story › simply-money-can-medi...

14.     Hospice Evaluation tools - psychometric properties of the Symptom Assessment Scale (SAS): https://pubmed.ncbi.nlm.nih.gov

15.     Palliative Performance Scale (PPS) and Palliative Care Conferences:  http://www.palliativealliance.ca › files › Physical Care › P..

16.     Memorial Symptom Assessment Scale Subscales https://www.midss.org › scoring_and_subscale_informatio

17.     20 Advantages and Disadvantages of Hospice Care - Vittana.org:  https://vittana.org › 20-advantages-and-disadvantages-of-

18.     Signs that the body is actively shutting down:  www.healthline.com/elderly/end-of-life

19.     Does a person know when they are dying?  https://www.medicinenet.com › article

20.     Five Physical Signs that Death is Nearing- https://besthospiceservices.com/five-physical-signs-that-death-is-nearing/

21.     A Guide To Understanding End-Of-Life Signs & Symptoms- https://www.crossroadshospice.com/hospice-resources/end-of-life-signs/